A Rainbow Somewhere

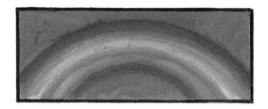

Written by Nancy Dowd

Illustrated by Mary Beth Schwark

"It's raining," said Jenny. "Will we see a rainbow today, Grandpa?"

"Maybe we'll see a rainbow today," said Grandpa. "But we won't see one yet."

"There is time to read a rainbow book,"
said Grandpa.

So Jenny and Grandpa read a
rainbow book.

"Rainbow books are okay," said Jenny.
"But when will we see a rainbow?"

"Maybe we'll see one today," said
Grandpa. "But we won't see one yet."

"There is time to make rainbow pictures,"
said Grandpa.

So Jenny and Grandpa made
rainbow pictures.

8

"Rainbow pictures are okay," said Jenny.
"But when will we see a rainbow?"

"Maybe we'll see a rainbow today," said
Grandpa. "But we won't see it yet."

"There is time to make rainbow popcorn
or rainbow cookies," said Grandpa.

So Jenny and Grandpa made
rainbow popcorn.

"Rainbow popcorn is okay," said Jenny.
"But when will we see a rainbow?"

"Maybe we'll see a rainbow soon,"
said Grandpa.

"Look, Jenny," said Grandpa. "Is it still raining, or did the rain stop?"

"It stopped raining, and the sun is out!"
said Jenny. "Will we see a rainbow,
Grandpa?"

"Maybe we will see a rainbow now," said Grandpa.

"There must be a rainbow somewhere,"
said Jenny. "Let's go look!"